This is Alfred.

Alfred is scared of a lot of things.

He's scared of things that go fast and of things that go slowly. Scared of falling, stumbling, dancing and using the telephone. Scared of saying the wrong thing when someone asks for directions. And of taking the bus on his own.

Alfred is scared of red light, thick duvets and fireworks. And of jumpers with tight necks.

But most of all, Alfred is scared of speaking in front of his class. That scares him more than anything else.

Luckily, Alfred has a long fringe. When he gets scared, he can hide behind it. He does that a lot. He feels safe behind his fringe.

It's Monday morning. The teacher is standing in front of the class with a big smile on her face.

"Each of you will be given a piece of paper with the name of an animal on it. You need to find something exciting to tell the class about that animal before Friday," she says.

Alfred's heart starts to pound. He pulls his fringe in front of his face. But it doesn't help. This is worse than falling, stumbling, dancing and using the telephone.

Alfred

and the Blue Whale

Mina Lystad

Illustrated by
Åshild Irgens

WACKÝ BEE

Worse than saying the wrong thing when someone asks for directions and taking the bus on his own put together. This is the worst thing ever. Speaking in front of his class.

The teacher puts a piece of paper on Alfred's desk. But Alfred doesn't dare read what it says. Instead, he crumples up the piece of paper, puts it in his bag and pretends it doesn't exist.

Alfred feels sick for the rest of the school day. He keeps thinking about having to speak in front of his class on Friday. It's five days until Friday. Five days is nothing.

He thinks about it all the way home. He thinks about it all the way through dinner.

Then Alfred goes to his room. He sits on his bed and pulls his fringe in front of his face.

I'll sit here forever, he thinks.

But forever is a long time. And it soon gets hot behind his fringe.

Alfred pushes it aside and looks out into his room.

His bag is on the floor. The piece of paper saying which animal he needs to talk about on Friday is in his bag. Perhaps he should look at it just once before going back to sitting on his bed forever.

Alfred finds the crumpled piece of paper.

He opens it and reads: BLUE WHALE.
The teacher has drawn a picture of a
smiling blue whale underneath. Alfred
doesn't smile.

Blue whale?

Alfred doesn't know anything about blue
whales. Well, he knows they're blue and
live in the sea. But nothing else.

I should try to find out more about blue whales, Alfred thinks. Just in case Mum and Dad don't let me sit here forever and I have to go to school on Friday.

Alfred goes to see his dad first.
"Do you know anything about blue whales?" he asks.
His dad looks up from his phone.

"They're very big," he says.

How big is very big? thinks Alfred. Bigger than a tree? Bigger than a tower block? Bigger than a plane? Bigger than a MOUNTAIN? BIGGER THAN THE MOON?

Next, Alfred goes to see his mum.
"Do you know anything about blue
whales?" he asks.
His mum stops pushing the pedals
of her exercise bike.

She wipes the sweat from her forehead
before answering.
"Blue whales sing to each other," she says.

Sing? Alfred thinks.
But blue whales live under water.
Don't they get water in their mouths
if they sing?

Alfred goes to see his sister who really likes reading and so has probably read a lot about blue whales. She probably knows how big they are and that they can sing.

"Annette, do you know anything about blue whales?" he asks.
But Annette doesn't have time to talk to him. She has a friend over. They're discussing important matters.

"Blue whales? You're such a baby! Don't bother us!" Annette yells, slamming the door.

Alfred goes back to his room and sits on his bed. He writes a list of what he knows so far:

Blue whales are blue.
They live in the sea.
They are very big (Dad says).
They can sing (Mum says).

Alfred looks at what he has written.
He needs to add more to the list.

Alfred goes down into the living room again. His dad finds a website about blue whales. There are so many amazing facts. Such as that blue whales are not fish, even though they live in the sea. They're mammals who need to come up to the surface to breathe.

Alfred reads that a blue whale's tongue weighs as much as an elephant. And that a blue whale's heart weighs as much as a car. Then he reads that blue whales sometimes swim very far all alone. How brave, Alfred thinks. He wonders whether blue whales also get scared.

Alfred reads more and more about blue whales as the week goes on. He reads that they used to live on land rather than in the sea. He reads that blue whales might be the biggest animal to have ever lived on Earth!

All week long Alfred reads so much about blue whales that he forgets how nervous he is. And every evening before he goes to bed he listens to blue whales singing to each other under water. There are recordings online.

But when Alfred wakes up on Friday morning, he suddenly feels nervous again. He can't even eat his breakfast.

He drags his feet on
the way to school.
His stomach hurts.

The teacher has written the names of everyone who is going to speak on the board. Alfred is almost last. He has a long time to think about how nervous he is.

Everyone who speaks is very clever and doesn't seem nervous at all. They talk about turtles, lions, parrots and foxes.

I'm going to be awful compared to everyone else, Alfred thinks.

But then he doesn't have any more time
to think, because suddenly it's his turn.
He walks up to the board.

Alfred looks down at his list.
The classroom is completely silent.

He looks at his class.
He looks at his teacher.
He pulls his fringe down over his eyes.

I can't do this, he thinks.
I'm going to faint.

Alfred takes a deep breath. Then he
closes his eyes and pictures a blue
whale. Sometimes they have to swim
very far all alone. That has to be much
scarier than this.

"Blue whales live in the sea," Alfred
mumbles.

He opens his eyes and peers out through
his fringe. The whole class is listening.
So far, so good.
Perhaps he should say something else.

"Blue whales can grow to be 34 metres long," Alfred continues.

Then something strange happens. The more Alfred reads, the better he feels. Suddenly Alfred forgets about everyone else in the classroom. He's just thinking about blue whales.

Alfred talks about how a blue whale's tongue weighs as much as an elephant. About how its heart weighs as much as a car. About how blue whales used to live on land rather than in the sea. About how they sometimes swim very far all alone.

To finish he pushes his fringe away from his face and mimics a blue whale singing. He hadn't even planned to do that.

Then Alfred is finished.
The teacher thanks him.
His classmates applaud.

He did it!
Alfred is so proud of himself.

He closes his eyes and pictures blue whales swimming around in the sea. It's almost as if they're pleased for him too.

He thinks about his talk all the way home.
He thinks about his talk all the way
through dinner. He thinks about his talk
until he goes to sleep.

But he doesn't think about his talk once
he's fallen asleep. Then he just dreams
about blue whales.

BLUE WHALE FACTS

1 The blue whale is the largest living creature on our planet. They can grow to over 30 metres long and weigh 140 tonnes. That's longer than three lorries put end to end and heavier than 115 giraffes.

2 Even a newborn baby whale is 8 metres long, which is the same length as a double-decker bus.

3 Blue whales can be found in all our planet's oceans except the Artic, usually swimming alone or in groups of two to four.

4 The oldest blue whale lived for around 100 years. However, normally their life span is about the same as a human's, so around 85 years.

5 Whales don't have teeth and they don't eat people! Instead, they have something called baleen plates, which are a bit like the bristles on a scrubbing brush.

6 Whales eat a tiny shrimp-like creature called krill. Because krill is bright orange, so too is a whale's poo!

7   Blue whales aren't able to breathe under water but they are able to hold their breath for up to 30 minutes. A single breath could inflate 2000 balloons, and when they breathe out they shoot water high up into the air through two blowholes.

8   Blue whales are the loudest animals in the world. Their hum is louder than a jet engine and can be heard up to 1000 miles away. They can hear each other but the frequency is too low for humans to hear without special equipment.

9   Blue whales can never go to sleep properly or they would drown. Instead, they take very short naps while swimming close to the ocean's surface. This is called logging.

10 Because blue whales used to be hunted and killed, it is thought that fewer than 10,000 remain worldwide. They are now a protected species and, in some places, their numbers are slowly growing. However, you could still sail the oceans every day for a year and never see a single one.

Published by

Wacky Bee Books
Shakespeare House, 168 Lavender Hill, London, SW11 5TG, UK

ISBN: 978-1-9999033-1-2

First published in the UK 2019

English translation © Siân Mackie 2019

This translation has been supported by NORLA.

Design by David Rose
Picture credits: Pixabay.com and Shutterstock.com

Printed and bound in the UK by AkcentMEDIA

www.wackybeebooks.com